YOUR KNOWLEDGE HAS VALUE

- We will publish your bachelor's and
  master's thesis, essays and papers

- Your own eBook and book -
  sold worldwide in all relevant shops

- Earn money with each sale

Upload your text at www.GRIN.com
and publish for free

Samuel Perrino Martínez

The concept of modernity in Moroccan press

GRIN Verlag

Bibliografische Information der Deutschen Nationalbibliothek:

Die Deutsche Bibliothek verzeichnet diese Publikation in der Deutschen National-
bibliografie; detaillierte bibliografische Daten sind im Internet über http://dnb.d-
nb.de/ abrufbar.

Imprint:

Copyright © 2012 GRIN Verlag GmbH
Druck und Bindung: Books on Demand GmbH, Norderstedt Germany
ISBN: 978-3-656-34664-7

MIDDLE EAST STUDIES
CULTURE AND RELIGION IN MIDDLE EAST

Research paper

The concept of modernity in Moroccan press

University of Southern Denmark

Student: Samuel Perrino Martínez

« Nous voyons se confronter deux tendances; avec leurs variations: une qui considère que l'idéologie religieuse s'oppose à la démocratie et à la modernité et prône la séparation de la religion et de l'Etat; l'autre qui invite la société à revenir à l'Islam comme source de légitimité et de régulation sociale, en tentant de le placer au centre des pratiques politiques[1] »
Mouna Hachin

Introduction

The concept of modernity and democracy has taken up many discussions in the Arab World. A constant feature is the debate as to whether or not the Arab or Islamic World is compatible with the idea of modernity, and understanding this idea from a Western perspective, in relation to a set of abstract values such as liberty or democracy.

The aim of this paper is mainly to attempt an analysis of the concept of modernity through the use of the French press in Morocco, concretely three newspapers: the "independents" Maroc-Hebdo, and " L'economiste" and the "officialist" Le Matin du Sahara et du Magheb,

The press is not just an interesting media due to the value it holds in providing information on world events, but also due to the fact that it reflects the opinions and points of view of the person, or the group behind the writing; therefore providing an interesting mirror of the society. The press has been chosen as a source in order to examine the Islamic or Arab vision of modernity. The discussion about the treatment of the concept "Modernity" in the Moroccan press is addressed through the evaluation of several questions:

The paper will mainly emphasize the concept of modernity; first talking about the general considerations of the concept in an abstract sense, then focusing on the main topics of discussion, and at last evaluating the paper of tradition in the modernizing initiative, distinguishing two different discourses.

---

[1] "We are in face of two trends : One, which consider the religious ideology is opposite to democracy and modernity, and it looks for the separation between State and Religion, and another which invites the society to go back to Islam as a source of legitimacy and social regulation, in order to place it in the centre of political practices".

This is a work basically descriptive, due to the characteristic of the sources (primary) which are not opportune for the interpretation. The work will intercalate the text with many quotes, referring to the discussed topic.

This work examines the existence of different perspectives on the same topic, through the treatment of the news and the language used. The paper will analyze different news between the years 2011 and 2012. It is mainly based in primary sources, however some secondary sources were also used as a theoretical framework.

Context

Press in Morocco

First, it is advisable provide a short analysis about the newspapers, and the general situation of press in Morocco.

Briefly, one can say the Moroccan press system is considered one of the most plurals inside Arab World (Jadidi, 2012), but it is true the Monarchy has an indirect control over press through grants and fines, which function is mainly to avoid questioning some type of issues that are almost untouchable (The Monarchy, the Sahara issue and the Religion).

This certain press plurality is visible through the numerous journals in Arabic and French which exist inside the country. According to the annual report of "Reporteros sin Fronteras" (Journalist without borders) Morocco has the 135 rank in Freedom of Press, in the overall world.

The main characteristic of the press analyzed here is that it is a "phrancophone" press, and for that reason, linked to an idea of cultural elite. In turn, it is reflected in a higher concern for politics and social topics, in opposition to Arab press, where in general, the news about events or sports have more relevance (Cooper, A.M).

This idea of elite is more remarkable if we consider that approximately 40 per cent of population is illiterate, and in addition, according to approximate estimations, only one per cent of Moroccan population usually read newspapers (Muñoz Ortega, 2012)

So, one may object, of course, according to these data that press is not representative of the real popular opinion, however there are several reasons why this journals may have a remarkable role.

As the journalist Inmaculada Szmolka points out (2006), the writing press is the communicational sector which has taken up one of the most important roles in the political evolution of the country in last years due to these ideas are sometimes a mirror to see the initiative of the modernist sectors of society. The newspaper media have placed a significant role in the process of political liberalization and transition to democracy.

Secondly, the role of the elite French press has a important power as generator of opinion, despite its small diffusion. Apart of that, we have to consider the characteristics of each journal to understand its importance.

Journals

The newspaper Le Matin du Sahara et du Magheb (The Morning of Sahara and Maghreb) is a diary newspaper, with a diffusion of 80.000 numbers each day. It is the officialist publication "par excellence" and its opinions reflected in a good way, the official opinion of Monarchy and the Makzhen[2] about different topics, both political and social, being considering almost as a official "propaganda organ" by some authors (Laparra Casado, M., 2007)

On the other hand, Maroc Hebdo journal is a weekly journal, with a diffusion of 20.000 numbers each week. It has an "independent editorial policy". The editorial group of this newspaper had serious problems with the Moroccan monarchy in the past, receiving the largest fine in the story of Moroccan press in 2008 However some authors consider this newspapers as part of official press; due to this incident the editorial policy became moderate in relation with go through the "red lines" of Moroccan press. It is a left-wing newspaper, and non alienated with any political party.

Lastly, L´economiste (The economist) is a diary journal, with a diffusion of 24.000 numbers each day. It is the journal of the economic elites. If it is true this

---

[2] The Makzhen is the governing elite in Morocco centred around the king and consisting of royal notables, businessmen, wealthy landowners, tribal leaders, top-ranking military personnel, security service bosses, and other well-connected members of the establishment.

journal is not critical with the Makzhen, it is one of the few French journals which is not directly or indirectly dependant upon any political party or the Monarchy in order to get its revenues. It is financed mainly through advertisement revenues.

Representativeness of the sample

Therefore, if it is true these newspapers are not representative of the whole Moroccan population, it is possible to say that they are representatives of the Moroccan elite in a some way. A Moroccan elite which are still conserve a high degree of influence, in different levels, as in a large part of the Arab world.

The selection is based on the possibility to use the digital archives and the linguistic accessibility, and the articles, in general were selected based on the relation with the treated topics, and the chronological proximity. Although the quoted articles in the paper are 15, the sample includes around 100 – 120 articles.

In this sense, the results displayed in this paper are limited to the selected media, and it is not possible to extrapolate, or generalize the data to whole Moroccan press. However these media are important speakers of the cultural elites of the country, so we can find some similarities and points in common.

Despite we are talking about a similar audience, we can find also different discourses in relation to modernity, which in general, has a positive value. It provides at the same time different perceptions, especially in relation with modernity and its relation with tradition, as we will see in the next pages.

The concept of modern

Definition

In first place, we are going to focus in the concept of modernity in Moroccan press, and the values related with it.

The Cambridge dictionary defines modernity as "the condition that results from being modern". In turn the word modern is defined as "designed and made using the most recent ideas and methods" (Cambridge).

.   These definitions do not clear up the concept, but they refer to an abstract concept. An abstract concept which, in turn is depending in a good way in the own values of the person or group.

As an example of the latter abstraction, the same concept can have different perspectives, even inside the cultures. For example, the jihad can have very different perceptions, from the need to preach Islam to peaceful ways to the need of doing the Holy War in the name of God, however it has a common and evident definition

That is why the concept of modernity does not have, or should not have the same value in the Islamic world than in the West, neither inside the own Arab world.

Comparison with Europe

One of the first general appreciations related with this topic is that the word "modernity" in Moroccan press, most of the time it is related with social and political issues, even though in the European newspapers is mainly related with cultural of historical issues. So, we find in the Moroccan press the modernity as a current topic, conceiving the issue as less abstract and closer in the second case.

Another main differences we find in order to distinguish the vision of Moroccan newspapers in relation to Europe is the characterization of modernization as a extremely positive idea unlike the neutral value that it use to be in the West. For example, a big part of the Government actions or social questions are defined inside the dichotomy modern / future, in spite of efficient / inefficient as in Europe. Therefore, it is usual see expressions such as a "modern reform", "modern laws", "modern country" or even, modern "people".

In the Western world the modern is linked with something new, without any type of moral value as good or bad. However in the Moroccan press we find a connotation related with the idea of advance or progress, with a strong positive sense.

Ideas linked to modernity

The idea of modernity, as I said above, as an abstract concept remind us a set of values, which can change with the time, and the context.

Basically, most of the ideas which are linked to the concept of modernity are referred to as "Western values", as democracy, technological advance, social advance, or fight against corruption, in the case of Morocco. However, it is possible to find a big difference to Europe, and that is the paper of tradition and religion, in this modern initiative.

Most of the associations with the word modernity are related with ideas of Politics an Society. In Politics the modernity is linked with democracy. It is remarkable the number of times these two words are joined in the same sentence *"Maroc n'a pas attendu ce jour pour s'inscrire dans une tradition démocratique exigeante et moderne"* [3](Anonymous, LM)

That democratization and modernization is generally related with a set of very different concerns of topics which one can classify, "grosso modo" in four aspects which we can consider the most remarkable: fight against corruption, new technologies, social change and linked with the latter religion.

Here, the most interesting is that in French press most of the values are referred to the Western idea of modernity, however, there is a basic point where we can distinguish this schemes, and that point is the different value given to tradition and religion in this vision of modernity.

As the main aim of the paper is a sociocultural perspective I will focus briefly in the first points, in order to develop, broadly, the role of Islam in the discourse of modernization.

On the matter of corruption, this is one of the factors with more importance, as a important brake for the modernity in Morocco, especially for the journal Maroc-Hebdo *"Cependant, le Maroc n'est pas à l'abri de certains maux qui freinent son développement économique d'un pays moderne ... Il y a aussi la persistance de la bureaucratie, renforcée par la corruption, qui réduisent quelque peu l'efficacité des efforts consentis en matière de dépenses sociales*[4]*"* (Amourag, 2011) However we find in most of the cases the journals do a vague critique, without names, and talking about "endemic illness" of Africa, or Arab world, in order to relatives the blame. In this aspect it is possible to see some kind of "internal censorship", due to this type of issues can annoy the Makzhen, one of the untouchable topics for press

The second most important concept linked to modernity is new technologies, which has a remarkable relevance in the recent Arab Spring. The new media appear

---

[3] Morocco does not wait today to be part of a democratic and modern tradition

[4] However, Morocco has not stop ceratains bad habits which brake its economic development as a modern county (...) There is still a remarkable bureocracy, which is butressing by the corruption, which reduce the efforts made in social expenses.

as a factor of change and social transformation to political level *"l'époque actuelle est propice au changement de cette pensée. Internet, SMS, Twitter, Facebook et le satellite sont en train de ré-usiner cette stable et vieille pensée des Maghrébins et des Arabes »* " [5] (Fahli, 2011)

At last, the other big field related with modernity is Human Rights, and Woman Rights, if it is true in this point it is possible to see certain differences referring to the treatment. Meanwhile the more independent press makes a brutal critique of the Moroccan society *"En effet, la femme marocaine est toujours battue. Ses droits fondamentaux sont bafoués. Elle est harcelée, violée et ce face au silence complice des autres. Pour certaines femmes, parler de harcèlement ou de viol équivaut à une mise au ban de la société. D'autres femmes subissent des "viols légaux" de la part de maris agressifs et violents"* [6] (Editorial, 2011), the "officialist" press, as to LM, makes an interpretation which stresses the achievements of Morocco in Human Rights or equality *"La paix, la tolérance, l'ouverture sur l'Autre et la coexistence interculturelle ont constitué les fondamentales du Maroc »* [7] (Anonymous, L´economiste) and,(this is a important difference that we are going to comment after) putting in relation with religious questions.

As we can see, most of the topics linked to modernity, or to be modern has no difference to what we can call a Western point of view (change of mentality from archaic positions, democratic laws, and political systems, new technologies etc...). So, therefore, the question is almost mandatory. Is the idea of modernity in Middle East conceived in the same way as in the West ? From the point of view of this paper the ideas present different characteristics, but if most of the topics and concerns are identifiable as Western, what is the difference?

---

[5] The current situation is opportune to the change of the mentalities: Internet, SMS, Twitter, Facebook and the satellite are changing completely this ancient way of thinking of the Arabs and people who lives in Maghreb

[6] In fact, the Moroccan woman is always battered. Her fundamental rights are violated. She is harassed, raped in front of the accomplice silence of the others. For some women, speaking about harassment or rape is the same as to be ostracized by the society. These women survive through legal violations for aggressive and violent husbands

[7] The peace, the tolerance, the openness to the Other, and the cultural coexistence have been the fundaments of Morocco"

The question of Modernity and Islam

According to the sociologist Anthony Giddens the progress to modernity is the big, or the main narrative of the current world. This idea of modernity shows up suddenly, tearing up the Ancient World from the moorings which used to have. It shows a completely new version of the world, which in turn, is in conflict with the tradition, and a sense of lost identity (Giddens, 1990).

Inside Arab, or Islamic World, this idea has more importance, due to, as to Fatima Mernissi says, the Islamic World has at the same time a problem of identity, a feeling of loosing identity, which in turn, makes it focus in the Past, and at the same time a feeling of decadence, which is necessary to mitigate looking to this idea of modernity, or even democracy (Mernissi, 2002).

That is why, in the Islamic world the relation of modernity and the relation with tradition is crucial, being this conflictive relation an important point of discussion in press *« Or dans les sociétés régies par des traditions et un droit de source divine, il subsiste des tensions, voire des oppositions frontales entre deux régimes de vérité, de justice et de légitimité: celui régi par la raison religieuse et celui plus récent de la raison philosophique et scientifique, devenue télé-techno-scientifique »* [8] (Hachim, 2011)

Inside the Moroccan press there are two different discourses in relation to this topic, and it is possible to see a so different treatment to this type of questions which is so interesting to comment.

One proof of the latter is see how religion is depicted in the different newspapers. Most of the time in the journals as Le Matin or L´economiste, when the press speaks about religion, they speak about religion and their relation with renovation of social values or the modernity itself, highlighting the complementary of this two fields, meanwhile the Maroc – Hebdo journal the questions about Islam are depicted in an aggressive and dual context, putting in the relation with news about Islamic fundamentalism or terrorism.

---

[8] Inside of our societies, ruled by the tradition and a Divine Right, there are still some tensions between two different systems of truth, justice and legitimacy : one which is based in the religious resason, and another based in the philosophy and scientific reason, which become techno-

The "conciliatory" vision

Most of the times, in the two first newspapers (LM, LE) it is remarkable to say that the word Islam is using as a tool to defend questions as Human Rights *« Par ailleurs, à y regarder de près, les principes de l'Islam ne sont pas différents de ceux des droits de l'Homme et de la démocratie »* (Fatehme, 2012)[9] or the women rights *« Le Islam a doté la femme d'une personnalité juridique indépendante, lui a reconnu le droit d'hériter, de gérer librement ses biens, de choisir son mari, de garder son nom de jeune fille, de divorcer. Il a limité le nombre des épouses jusque-là illimité et a soulagé Eve de la culpabilité de la chute du paradis, devenue œuvre aussi bien de l'homme que de la femme dans le Coran »*[10] (Fakhraie, 2012)

However, they "recognize" that sometimes, it can exist a certain incompatibility or sometimes, it can be seem as opposite to Islam, this is due to a misinterpretation of Islam, by "forces" who want to came back to the past. In the articles they point out the revolutionary, and innovator power of Islam, as a great force to modernity.

From this conciliatory perspective there are several interesting articles as one with the title "Is it possible to be feminist and Muslim ?" where the own author begin to define herself as feminist and Muslim at the same time, to finish saying that Islam and feminism have in common a strong sense of social justice *"Beaucoup pensent que les deux notions sont incompatibles. En réalité, en tant que musulmane féministe, je pense qu'elles ont bien plus en commun qu'on ne l'imagine, surtout en matière de justice sociale*[11] *»* (Alaoui, 2012).

In the same way others authors point out the feminist content of Islam in order to get the equality, saying that there are numerous examples in the Quran where Muhamad which established important rights for women"*Tous les dysfonctionnements, défauts, discriminations, mépris de la femme et violations de*

---

[9] The principles of Islam are not so different than the Human Rights and democracy.

[10] The Islam has given to the women one juridical personality, it has given the right to inherit, the right to manage with freedom her goods, the right to choose her husband, the right to keep her name in the name of her small daughter, and the right to ask for divorce. It has narrow the number of wives, and it has forgiven Eve from the guilt of Paradise, which was an action, with the same responsibility, both men and women

[11] Many people think that this two notions are incompatible. In fact, as to feminist Muslim. I think they have a lot of things in common, especially in the matter of social Beaucoup pensent que les deux notions sont incompatibles. En réalité, en tant que musulmane féministe, je pense qu'elles ont bien plus en commun qu'on ne l'imagine, surtout en matière de justice sociale

ses droits ayant affecté ce genre pendant des siècles résultent de préjugés attribués à l'Islam, des us, coutumes et traditions et d'une culture populaire controuvée, ne reposant sur aucun des fondements de l'Islam, outre la mauvaise interprétation des textes et l'extrémisme religieux »[12] (Lansari, 2012)

As mentioned prior, it is so notable that most of the articles with "religious content" refer to ideas considered, as we saw before as modern (Human Rights, women, even freedom of speech) , and therefore trying to remark the complementary of both realities, with a strong social component.

On other hand, there is few references to an analysis of the religious texts, in a personal sense. This type of recommendations are focused in this way, if it is true that Le Matin has a special section to the commentary of Quran,

Apart from that, in this journals, it possible to see different discussions about the relation between science and Islam, remarking that Islam does not suppose any problem for the science research, but the opposite, using again an Islamic argumentation to understand the relation between science and religion *"Aujourd'hui, le Coran nous parle le langage du 21e siècle : celui de la science et de la technologie, celui du savoir et du droit ! Le mot «science» et ses dérivées sont cités dans le Coran 811 fois, contre 14 fois seulement pour le mot «prière», 14 fois pour le jeûne, 13 fois pour «Al Hajj» (le pèlerinage), et 32 fois pour la «Zakat»*[13]*»* (Hachim, 2010)

However, the articles where it is more evident to see the refusal of the dichotomy Islam and tradition / modernity are the articles of opinion where the authors ask for a "fair middle point"   , avoiding extremism extremely linked, "in a bad way" to the past or the future *"s'accrocher à une lecture sclérosée de la religion et rejeter la modernité, ou, au contraire, se conformer totalement à la*

---

[12]All the malfunctions, mistakes, discrimination, offenses if the women, and violation of her rights have affected this sex during centuries, giving as a result a lot of prejudices attributed to Islam, due to the habitude, the tradition and from a popular culture, which was not based in any rule of Islam, but in a wrong interpretation of the Scriptures

[13] Today, the Quran Speaks us the language of the 21 century, the language of the science and technology, the language of the wisdom and the Right ! The word "science" is quoted 811 times in Quran, for 14 times the word « prayer », 13 times the word pilgrimage, and 32 times the word Zakat

réalité et dénigrer la religion. Ces deux risques sont dus au fait que la pensée est devenue stérile [14]» (L,economiste, 2012)

Therefore, one permanent idea in this argument is giving the Islam, not necessarily as something from the past, but as a identity which is also necessary to check out in all moment, in base to a modern conceptions in permanent revision *"Il s'en suivrait un dialogue de sourds, si ce n'est la sincérité de l'engagement et la volonté de construire positivement nos sociétés à défaut de dissiper tous les malentendus, interrogeant de part et d'autre la dérive d'un humanisme soumis à la modernité, prêchant parfois par élitisme et de l'autre côté un système de pensée enchaîné à la tradition non exempt de sa part de populisme"* [15] (Arkoum, 2012).

Ultimately, we find a vision which claims, in all the moment, harmonize tradition and modernity, and, which consider possible, using a "guiddensian language" be able to advance through modernity, without lost the moorings of tradition, "making modern" the tradition, in some way.

The "confronted" vision

Otherwise, in the Maroc-Hebdo the religion is depicted, according to this point of view, in a very different way.

At first, the world Islam in this newspaper is associated, most of the times with Islamic fundamentalism, depicting a big concern about this topic, and pointing out as a big threat.

It is so curious see how, in this point the pictures that appear in each journal related with Islamic fundamentalism. In Maroc-Hebdo one find pictures of religious leaders, with weird sights, pointing with the finger to the air, and threatening look, giving an aspect almost dehumanized and grotesque, which is in a contrast with the pictures displayed in the other two journals about the same topic, with pictures associated to mosques, Scriptures… Therefore one can see the big contrast between a set of pictures which transmitted in a visual effect, feelings completely different.

---

[14] Putting uo in a extreme vision of religion, refusing the modernity, or in the opposite side, refusing and criticize the religions This two risks make the thinking completely useless

[15] It, s no way, if the sincerity of our engagement and the willing to built in a positive way all the misunderstandings, , Questioning one part and the other the drift of a humanism subjected to modernity, with this elitist characterization, and on the other side, a system of thought chained to tradition with its part of populism

Moreover, in Maroc-Hebdo it highlights the enormous threat which supposes to the advance of the country, the plans of the terrorist groups (in opposition with the others newspapers which always highlight the idea of minority about this groups), speaking about plans as create the United States of the Maghreb.

In order to show the message of "complementary between Islam and modernity" in LE and LM, when they speak about this topics, they highlight the socioeconomic factors which create this situation of extremism inside some sectors of the population, at the same time, they emphasize the wrong interpretation of Islam for this (Najib, 2012) [16]"

In MH is also mentioned this socioeconomic motivations, however in spite of compare to the positive values of Islam, as LE or LM, the comparison is with the tolerant values of the Moroccan Kingdom , and not religion.

For other part, going back to the issue of women rights or human rights, in MH does not appear the Islamic allegation, but the allegation is made by a certain idea of rationality or progress, if it is true it does not do any type of critique to religion or religion values.

The most remarkable when MH speaks about that topic is, the journal invoke civic values, or "Modern conceptions" as the idea of citinzenship, the own idea of modernity , or the importance of the law (Le Code de la Familie), and not the idea of "Islamic equality" as in the other journals *"Comme le souligne l'Association démocratique des Femmes du Maroc, il est évident qu'en dépit des avancées, l'accès des Marocaines à la citoyenneté pleine et entière n'est pas encore acquis[17]"* (Najib, 2011)

Another notable difference is in the emphasis given to the associations and NGO,s as an elements of awareness, instead of religious authorities, *« efforts du mouvement féministe marocain (intellectuels –hommes et femmes-, société civile, volonté politique) si cette étape affronte courageusement les causes des difficultés*

---

[16] For several attempts to denaturalize the Islam in general, and Quran in particular for the Machiavellian methods, which isolated everything from the general context

[17] As the Democratic Association of Moroccan Women point our, it is evident, despite the advance, the access to the complete citizenship by the Moroccan women is not already get it

de l'application du Code de la Famille, nous pourrons tous arriver à des Solutions [18]» (Najib, 2011).

Therefore, it is possible to see, if it is true both discourses insist in the idea of modernity, the type of associations and the message is considerably different, both the Woman Rights, and the treatment of Islamic fundamentalism

However, it is necessary to remark this conciliatory speech is also present sometimes in MH, existing some articles which speak also, about the necessity to conciliate Islam and, for example democracy *"si les principes et les valeurs prônés par l'Islam sont éternelles, nous avons besoin de moderniser nos institutions politiques et même sociales, nos traditions, nos systèmes. Un véritable "Etat islamique" doit être démocratique car il reçoit sa légitimité du peuple, il est responsable devant lui et travaille pour servir et protéger les droits de tous ses citoyens. Toute autre forme de gouvernement serait oppressive, et donc non-islamique ».*[19] (Masnoudi, 2011) however, the editorial policy is mainly, for other way, displaying an idea of progress which is not inevitably linked to tradition.

Conclusion

The results presents in this paper are, in a some way a simplification of the total amount of articles processed, but, it looks for find out a set of guidelines and points in common, in order to characterize the idea of modernity.

Therefore, I conclude that, if it is true there is an unanimity to identify the values associated to modernity to something positive and linear, it is meaningful points out that there are two differentiated discourses in relation to religion as driving force of change or not, depending of the consulted newspapers.

Therefore, we distinguish between a conciliator discourse, which understands religion is a complement, and even an accelerator of modernity, which appear in journals as "Le Matin" or "L'economiste", and a confrontational or differentiated

---

[18] Efforts of the feminist Moroccan movement (intelligentsia – both men and women – civil society, political willingness-,) if this new step face in a courageous way the reasons of the difficult application of the Family Code, we can arrive to solutions.
[19] If the rules and the premises of Islam are eternal, we have to modernize our political institutions and even, social structures, our traditions, and our systems. A truth Islamic State should be democratic, and recognize its legitimacy in the people, and serve to protect the rights of all the citizens. Another type of Government would be oppressive, and therefore, non-Islamic

discourse, in which the idea of religion is not necessarily linked with the idea of modernity.

The fact there are different discourses inside the Francophone press in Morocco, also depicts, the enormous internal diversity which exists inside the Islamic world. A vision which is sometimes simplify due to simplistic or Manichean perspectives.

"To begin with, I should not judge Islam. Each Muslim practices a different Islam, believe in the same God, but they can choose a different way to reach Him"
Pedro Antonio de Alarcón (1833-1891) Spanish writer

REFERENCES

Primary sources:

- **Alaoui M´daghri, Abdelkebin** (April, 29th, 2012) Il n´y a pas distinction entre l´homme et la femme. Le Matin du Sahara et du Maghreb
- **Amourag, A.** (February 19th, 2011) : Les grands atouts de l'économie marocaine en 2010. Maroc-Hebdo International
- **Anonymous** (March, 5th, 2012) Islam, le Maroc veut faire tomber les prejugués. L´economiste
- **Arkoun, Mohamed** (September, 1st, 2011) : Recherche la verité, faillibilité des maitres. Peut-on reformer en Islam ?. Le Matin du Sahara et du Maghreb
- **Belghazi, Naoufal** (May, 21st, 2011) Islam contre fanatisme. L´economiste
- **Editorial** (October, 23rd, 2011) Le Maroc, terre de paix et tolérance. Le Matin du Sahara et du Maghreb
- **Editorial**, (February, 18th, 2011) Le Maroc dans le sillage des réformes. Le Matin du Sahara et du Maghreb
- **Fahli, Driss** (January, 21st, 2011) Tout change et rien ne bouge. Maroc-Hebdo International
- **Fakhraie, Fatemeh** (January, 13rd, 2012) Etre musulmane et féministe n´est pas incompatible. Le Matin du Sahara et du Maghreb
- **Hachim, Moina** (December, 13rd, 2010) Islam, medias et bidomages, ou la vision monolitique fantasmée. L´economiste
- **Hachim, Moina** (December, 13rd,, 2011) Islam, politique et querelle des Anciens et des Modernes. L´economiste
- **Lansari, Mohamed** (March, 18th, 2012) Coran, science et modernité. Le Matin du Sahara et du Maghreb
- **Masnoudi, Radwan** (December 19th, 2011) Le Maroc peut changer la mauvaise image du monde musulman. Maroc-Hebdo International
- **Najib, Abdelhak** (March 12nd, 2010) Journée de la femme au Maroc. De qui se moque-t-on. Maroc Hebdo International
- **Najib, Abdelhak** (March, 16th, 2012) La bataille pour l´égalité est encore longue. Maroc-Hebdo International

Secondary sources

- **Alvarado, David** (2004) El Islam ante la modernidad, El Siglo n 673
- **Cooper, Anne Messerly** (1982): French-Language Newspapers in the Arab World: An Elite Press, paper presented at the annual meeting of the International Communication Association
- **Giddens, Anthony** (1990): The Consequences of Modernity, Standford, Standford University Press.
- **Jadidi, Said** (2012): Libertad de prensa en Marruecos: un éxito de curiosidad from
  http://www.marruecosdigital.net/xoops/modules/wfsection/article.php?articleid= 3480
- **Laparra Casado, Daniel; Penalva Verdú, Clemente Antonio; Mateo Pérez, Miguel Ángel** (2007): La imagen de España y Marruecos durante el incidente del islote de Perejil. Revista CIDOB d´afers internacionals, N 79
- **Mernissi, Fatima** (2002): Islam and democracy, fear of the modern world. New York. Basic Books.
- **Muñoz Ortega** (2012) Marruecos y los medios de comunicación from http://latitud194.com/?p=1537
- **Reporteros sin Fronteras** (2010) *Informe de libertad de prensa 2010*
- **Szomolka, Inmaculada** (2006): Los medios de comunicación en el proceso de cambio político en Marruecos, *in PÉREZ BELTRÁN, Carmelo*. Sociedad civil, derechos humanos y democracia en Marruecos. *2006. Universidad de Granada, Granada*